G'D...
TEACH Y...
AUSTR...
IN 20 EASY LESSONS

COLIN BOWLES

G'DAY!
TEACH YOURSELF
AUSTRALIAN
IN
20 EASY LESSONS

illustrated by Louis Silvestro

HarperCollins*Publishers*

A TV interviewer in 1974 asked Mark Tonelli what Princess Anne had said when she presented him with the gold medal for the 100m backstroke at the Commonwealth Games in Christchurch. Tonelli replied: "I couldn't understand her. She speaks English and I speak Australian."

HarperCollins*Publishers*
77–85 Fulham Palace Road,
Hammersmith, London W6 8JB

This paperback edition 1993
1 2 3 4 5 6 7 8 9

First published in Great Britain by
Angus & Robertson Publishers (UK) 1987
Reprinted six times

Copyright © Colin Bowles 1986

The Author asserts the moral right to
be identified as the author of this work

ISBN 0 00 638344 0

Set in California

Printed in Great Britain by
Hartnolls Ltd, Bodmin, Cornwall

Contents

Introduction

A popular misconception among foreign travellers first visiting Australia's brown and unpleasant land is that because they can speak English they can get by Down Under. This is patently untrue.

The real position was recognised as early as 1945 by the then Minister of Immigration, the late Arthur Calwell, who said: "All newcomers of course will have to learn to speak Australian." It was confirmed in 1982, when the Australian Film Commission was invited to show several Australian films at the Miami Film Festival in Florida — as long as they carried English sub-titles.

There has been a chasm forming between the Mother Tongue and its bastard offspring ever since the first convicts arrived at Port Jackson, and the chasm is growing wider. Today a Londoner stepping out of the cocoon of a British Airways 747 at Sydney's Mascot Airport will probably have the same trouble understanding what's said to him as he would have had if the plane had landed in Paris or Ouagadougou. He'll need a phrase-book — and here it is.

Loud and raucous, down-to-earth and colourful, the Australian language combines the worst and best of the Australian character. But the richness of the language can only be truly appreciated by the student when experiencing the ebb and flow of everyday conversation. To simulate this experience, this book presents, in addition to sections on Basic Australian, a series of Instant Conversations, featuring a fictional working class family called the Fosters. This family is a product of the author's imagination, bears no similarity to anyone living or dead etc., and is to be found everywhere throughout the sunburnt country. Look at the conversations, study the accompanying vocabulary, and you'll soon get a feel for the Australian idiom. But to achieve a fluency which will make you incomprehensible anywhere outside Australia itself, you must also learn to imitate the pronunciation and rhythm of the native speaker. The rules follow: use them while reading the Instant Conversations aloud, and you'll be omen osed (see p.54).

Diction

The secret of good Australian diction is to speak as fast as possible, slurring, or avoiding altogether, the more common words, and never enunciating syllables. Try not to open the mouth.

For example, if you are going to ask someone if they are going to have a shower, you don't say:

"Are you going to have a shower?"

Correct Australian is:

"Yagunna avashowr?"

It has been suggested that Australians speak so rapidly because of the prevalence of flies. It may also be born of a desire not to waste valuable drinking time. Whatever the reason, it's important to learn the art.

This is especially true of interrogatives. For example:

"Why don't you" must be pronounced "Whinecha", or "Wadoancha".

"Why didn't you" becomes "Wadincha".

"What does he" becomes "Wotssy" or even "Wossy".

The last example above is a case of the disappearing "do". The verb "to do" is cumbersome and has largely been obliterated from the language without in any way affecting meaning. For example:

"Do you want a drink?" becomes "Jerwannadrink?"

"Did you go to the beach?" becomes "Jergoda the beach?"

"Did you hear about Gary?" becomes "Jerebout Gazza?"

"I didn't know it was raining" becomes "I dint note was rainin."

Australian speech is about economy and brevity. You will note in the example above I have put no apostrophe next to the last letter in "rainin". This is because the "g" has not been left off the word. In Australian it does not exist.

As a general rule, remember that if a "d", "t" or "g" comes at the end of a word, with a consonant in front of it, it ceases to exist. Example:

"It's yaw shout. I gotta las bleedin roun."

Note: There are only 25 letters in the Australian alphabet. The aspirate "h" is never used. Thus the famous Australian directive "Pull your head in" is spoken as "Pullyeredin". And the pronoun "he" becomes simply "e" or "y". For the sentence "He won, didn't he?" say "E won, dinty?"

The rapid-fire speech pattern does not hold true for short sentences. The trick is that all Australian sentences are the same length, so that a sentence of 20 words has the same duration as one with only two. If you want to say "fair go" for example, you should take approximately five seconds over it.

Finally, remember that inflection and stress are always on the last syllable of any speech, and the pitch rises as if you were asking a question. The best way to attain this effect is to stand in front of a mirror and goose yourself at the end of each sentence. It is advisable to practise this exercise in private.

Vowels

The Australian accent is heavily influenced by the environment and the local sounds. In the case of Australia those sounds are the sheep, the crow and the galah. A case in point is the vowel, often written as "a", which is always pronounced "aa", as in "baastard" and "baandry". The exact sound produced cannot adequately be reproduced in print but it is similar to a sheep being strangled with a piece of piano wire. You can practise this sound yourself by pulling down your underwear and sitting on a sharp stick with an ice cube clamped between the knees. Say "baastard" over and over while you repeat the process. Practice makes perfect.

The peculiarities of Australian vowel production become more noticeable as you move away from urban areas into the country. Accents become broader and harsher. "I" sounds become "oi" and "I like" becomes "Oi loike". "Off" becomes "orf", "salt" becomes "solt" and "shower" broadens into "share".

For example, if a farmer comes down from the country to spend a few days at Bondi, has a swim and wants to have a shower to get the salt off, he will say:

"Oi reckon oil avashare nare an getta solt orf."

Another feature of the broader rural accent is that "u" sounds have a tendency to become "ar". "Stuck" becomes "stark". I once saw a farmer get his fingers caught in a piece of machinery. Pleas for assistance were prefixed with: "Faark, me yans stark!"

In the bush you will also hear "day" pronounced "die". (As in the famous World War II joke in which a British officer approached an Australian soldier at Tobruk and asked him if he had come to die. The soldier said no, he had come yesterdie.)

However, this practice is not as widespread as is generally thought, and is probably most common in Monty Python sketches featuring people called Bruce. (It's also common in Earls Court, London, where expatriate Australians do things to their language they would never dream of doing at home.)

That gives you a general grounding on Australian pronunciation. There is lots more to learn, and this will be explained in the following pages. Meanwhile, do your exercises and practise speaking all your sentences with your teeth firmly clenched, making your vowels pass through the nose. Take five seconds over everything you say.

Good luck.

The Family

Meet the Foster family. Mr Foster is a battler. His name is Les. He lives in Darlo. He works as a garbo. He wants to win the Lotto.

Mrs Foster is the old cheese. Her name is Maureen. She spends most of her time watching soapies on the idiot box. Next week she is going into hospital for a re-bore. Les thinks she's as silly as a two bob watch. She wants to be like Ita Buttrose.

Shane is the son of Mr and Mrs Foster. Shane is a dole bludger. He's always boracic. Mr Foster reckons he's a deadhead and he wouldn't work in an iron lung. He spends most of his time down at Bondi riding waves. He wants to get rid of his zits.

Darlene is the daughter of Mr and Mrs Foster. Darlene is a top sort. She comes across for some of Shane's mates in the back of their bog wagons. She works as a check-out chick in Coles. Her room is always a bit of a brothel. She wants to be a surfie groupie.

The Fosters have a pet dog called Scungeball. It's a bitser.

The Foster family are up to their eyes in hock. They used to live in a unit in Bondi but they got turfed out. So now they live in a grotty terrace in Darlo, two bedrooms and a sleep-out.

Do you want to know more about the Foster family? Then you must begin the lesson now.

Vocabulary

battler
someone who gamely attempts to make ends meet each week despite overwhelming odds

Darlo
Darlinghurst. One of the less salubrious suburbs of Sydney. Hangout for Neeshies (Orange People), punks, and trendies who are slumming it. Hardly any of these people actually have to live there

garbo
(short for "garbologist") a refuse collector

Lotto
lottery

old cheese
mother of the family unit. (Also referred to as "the old chook".)

soapies
serialised TV dramas; the staple cultural diet of most Australians

re-bore
a hysterectomy

Ita Buttrose
glamorous former editor of the *Australian Women's Weekly* and a celebrated over-achiever

dole bludger
one who is content to live off social security payments (by contrast with one who is genuinely unemployed and is looking for work)

boracic
without money

deadhead
a good-for-nothing

Bondi
a jungle of red brick rented flats, New Zealand dope dealers, house breakers, surfies and Japanese tourists — oh, and a surf beach

zits
pimples

top sort
an attractive young woman

to come across
to bestow sexual favours
bog wagon
a panel van, with a dashboard lined with imitation fur. The back of the van is generally fully carpeted and even the most rusted-out model will have a top of the range stereo system with graphic equaliser and quadraphonic sound. There is always a mattress in the back. (Also "shaggin wagon".)
check-out chick
(term still used in some areas, now slightly dated) a girl who works a cash desk in a supermarket
bit of a brothel
a mess
surfie groupie
a girl who sleeps with as many surfing celebrities as possible
bitser
a dog of undetermined pedigree, i.e. a mongrel
up to one's eyes in hock
having used up all of one's available credit and then some; an extreme form of poverty
unit
home unit. This means a flat. (Known as a "condominium" in the US.)
turfed out
asked to vacate the premises
grotty
run-down and/or dirty
terrace
a terraced house
sleep-out
a rear porch that has been converted to an extra bedroom with the use of asbestos walls

Exercises

1. Form a sentence using the word "Ita Buttrose".
2. Should Shane squeeze his zits or buy a lotion?
3. What do you think is Darlene's attitude towards the philosophical position of Hume and Locke?
4. Give an example of a top sort you know. What is her phone number?

Obsoletes

Thanks to Paul Hogan and Barry Humphries, many foreigners think Australia is the land where the one-eyed trouser snake is king. Thus immigrants and visitors often make idiots of themselves by using words and phrases long obsolete or restricted to the stage performances of Dame Edna Everage.

When an Australian goes to urinate, for example, he most often goes for a piss, a slash, or a leak. He hardly ever shakes hands with the wife's best friend, syphons the python or points Percy at the porcelain, unless it's late at night and he's feeling jocular and it is understood that he's doing an impersonation of Les Patterson.

He may be lucky enough to get a good root but he never spears the bearded clam or threads the eye of the golden doughnut. He might do "the dirty deed", but not to his wife. He'll play "hide the sausage" with anyone, provided they're female. Even popular Bazzerisms like "driving the porcelain bus", "shouting down the great white telephone", or "having a Technicolour yawn" are rare. Most good Australians just "chuck up" and carry on drinking.

Australians no longer call each other "sport" or "cobber". If you hear someone say "sport" to you, you can be sure that the speaker is not in a good mood. "Sport" is now used as a signal word and a threat, as in "Watch it, sport". Older Australians may sometimes talk of their old cobbers in the army, but younger Australians find the expression quaint. "Digger", too, is reserved for members of the Returned Servicemen's League, and is normally only heard on Anzac Day, usually in the same reverent breath as the word "Gallipoli".

Old advertising copywriters, trying to appeal to C2 housewives, sometimes use "bonzer" but you'll rarely hear it spoken. "Ridgey-didge"—meaning true or 100% guaranteed—is also almost obsolete.

Australians no longer come the raw prawn and, above all, they are not all still called Bruce and Sheila. Australians today are called Shane and Mario and Con and Kylie and Maria.

Blokes are still blokes, except to girls, when they're guys, but girls are hardly ever sheilas. They're tarts.

2

In the Disco

Shane and his friend Macka are going to the disco. They put on their best strides and a new pair of jocks. They are hoping to crack on to some tarts and do a bit of good for themselves. Shane is Stone Motherless but has put the bite on his old man for ten bucks. They drive to the disco in Macka's old bomb.

Instant Conversation

SHANE: What a top sort.

MACKA: Where?

SHANE: The one over there with the blonde hair and the big norks.

MACKA: Wooden mine givin that one. She's with some turkey.

SHANE: The smooth bastard with the mo?

MACKA: Winecha go over an see if ya can white ant im?

(Later.)

MACKA: Wossa matter? Dip out?

SHANE: Yeah. Put the ard word onner an she told me ter rack off.

MACKA: Probly a lezzo.

7

SHANE:	Think I'll it the toe.
MACKA:	What about we try an con up those two tarts inner corner?
SHANE:	Nar, I've ad the bomb. You kickin on?
MACKA:	Not stayin ere on me pat, ya bloody piker. Miteswell come with ya.
SHANE:	This place is up the shit. Goda Selina's nex time.

They hop in Macka's car but they're not even out of the car park when it dies in the arse. They have to leg it home and they don't get in till sparrowfart.

Vocabulary

strides
trousers or jeans
jocks
underpants (Sometimes known as "duffies" or "undies".)
to crack on to
to make acquaintance with
tart
any female, regardless of her sexual reputation
to do a bit of good for oneself
to score with a person of the opposite sex
Stone Motherless
totally and absolutely. In this instance the word "broke" is understood, but the phrase can also be used with the word "last", to describe the performance of the horse you had your money on
to put the bite on
to borrow from (Also "put the touch on".)
old man
father
old bomb
a car of ancient vintage
norks
breasts
wooden mine
an expression of interest. The things usually found in wooden

mines are prurient desire and hope of financial gain
to give it one
(usually preceded by a "wooden mine") to perpetrate sexual
intercourse
turkey
someone so ineffectual as not to warrant being labelled a
"bastard"
mo
a moustache. Almost always worn in the Lillee style, growing
down the side of the mouth to create an impression of
toughness. Common among health club attendants, used car
salesmen and beach inspectors
to white ant
to cut in on someone else's property or territory by means of
subterfuge or sabotage (From the Australian wood-eating
white ant, i.e. termite.)
to dip out
not to meet with success
to put the hard word on
to make a proposition of a sexual nature
to rack off
to depart. Normally used as an imperative, as in "Rack off,
hairylegs"
probly
most likely
lezzo
a lesbian; anyone who declines your sexual advances (Also
"lesbo".)
to hit the toe
to leave
to con up
to dazzle someone with the full array of your charms
to have had the bomb
to be exhausted
to kick on
to continue, usually in reference to drinking or partying
on me pat
on my own (Rhyming slang: Pat Malone=own.) When you're
in this position, you're said to be "standing round like a shag
on a rock"

piker
someone who ruins someone else's fun by going home or leaving early
miteswell
given the situation I think it will be best to
up the shit
not any good
Selina's
at time of writing, a popular nightspot in Coogee
to die in the arse
to break down
to leg it
to walk
sparrowfart
dawn

Exercises

1. Express the Australian male's attitude to women, as presented by Shane and Macka, in less than 10 words.
2. What do you think of Shane's ability to con up tarts? Answer yes or no.
3. (a) Have you ever dipped out with a tart? (b) If you answered "yes" write out "I must learn to bullshit" 100 times.
4. Make up a sentence using the words "Ita Buttrose", "norks" and "rack off".
5. Do you think Macka is a homosexual? If so, why? (Answer very carefully.)

How and When to Use the Word "Bastard"

Correct usage of the word "bastard" is perhaps one of the hardest aspects of the language to learn. A term of endearment (as in "Owyagowin, y'old bastard") or of abuse (as in "You rotten bastard!"), it is most often used simply as a synonym for "person". But as a rule, you don't call someone you don't know a "bastard", as the subtle shades of meaning can be misconstrued.

In describing other people, anyone and everyone is a bastard, unless they're female. If you like someone, they're not a bad bastard, and if you feel sorry for them they're a poor bastard. If you don't like them, they're that bastard and if you don't like them and despise them as well they're that mongrel bastard.

If you don't like them, but you're a bit frightened of them, they're a bad bastard. If they're smart, they're a clever bastard. If they're not, they're a dozey bastard. If they wear their lechery on their sleeves they're a grubby bastard and if they're indolent, they're a lazy bastard. If they have a malevolent streak, they're a nasty bastard. If they have no manners they're a rude bastard. If they're miserly, they're a lousy bastard.

Other popular bastards are unlucky bastards, queer bastards, officious bastards and weak bastards.

The Australian language is built around the bastard. Learn the word, say it correctly, use it wisely. Remember — every Australian is some sort of bastard, but you only say it to his face when you know him well enough to have shouted each other drinks. (More of that later.)

13

How to Bullshit

Sundy arvo Shane goes down the pub. He meets Gazza.
Gazza is a bit of a nong. Gazza shouts Shane a middy and
Shane decides to try and make a big man of himself.

Instant Conversation

GAZZA: You look rooted. Ard night?

SHANE: Yeah, been on the nest all night.

GAZZA: Lucky bastard.

SHANE: Just some blonde tart I conned up at Selina's.
Top sort.

GAZZA: Shit eh?

SHANE: Yeah, all over me like a rash, she was.

GAZZA: Dead set?

SHANE: Got a flat in Coogee. Raced me off soon as we
got in the door. Oastie with Qantas. Rooted
er silly all night.

GAZZA: Owsyerotten form?

SHANE: That's not all. Whenner mate comes ome she
godder gear off and jumped in the cot too.
Shoulda seen the bod on it!

(Macka enters.)

14

GAZZA:	Eh, Macka . . . Shane reckons egod is end in larse night.
MACKA:	Pig's arse! E was with me an egot what I got. Sweet bugger all!
GAZZA:	Eh?
MACKA:	Wise up, Gazza. E sucked ya in again, dinty? E coulden lie straight in bed, the bastard!

Vocabulary

Sundy
Sunday
arvo
afternoon
Gazza
Australian form of "Gary"
nong
a dim-witted person
middy
a measured glass of beer (See Basic Australian: Pubs.)
to make a big man of oneself
to raise one's personal prestige in the eyes of others. This usually involves boasting or "skiteing"
rooted
tired (Also "bushed" or "shagged out".)
on the nest
performing acts of a sexual nature
shit eh?
a meaningless expression used to denote surprise or wonderment. Can also be used in a mundane way when there is nothing else to say. If you go to the hotel in Ceduna in South Australia and walk into the public bar you'll find it full of people saying "Shit eh?" and nothing else
all over someone like a rash
unable to keep one's hands off someone, owing to one's extreme sexual attraction to that person
dead set?
is that right? Another expression of wonderment. Can also be used to emphasise a point, meaning you're telling the

Gospel truth. You probably aren't (Also "straight up".)

to race off
to urgently place someone in an appropriate horizontal position, ready to receive your sexual favours

oastie
(literally "hostie") an air hostess. All female flight attendants are suspected of being nymphomaniacs ("nymphos") by Australian males. All male flight attendants, on the other hand, are known to be gay

to root someone silly
to have frequent sexual intercourse with someone over a short period

owsyerotten form?
(literally "how's your rotten form?") roughly translates as "some people have all the luck"

gear
clothes

the cot
bed

bod
the female form, as displayed by a top sort. Usually accompanied by a "nice set"

to get one's end in
to succeed in seducing a female

pig's arse!
general expression of contempt; standard response to any form of bullshit (Also can be abbreviated to "pig's!". Milder form is "Drop off!".)

sweet bugger all (See note overleaf)
nothing

wise up
a request to raise the level of one's intelligence

sucked in
duped

dinty?
is that not correct?

he couldn't lie straight in bed
cliche expression, denoting that a certain person is pathologically dishonest

Exercises

1. What do you think of Gazza's intelligence? (Extra sheets of paper are available at the front desk.)
2. Practise your bullshitting. Stand in front of a mirror and bullshit to yourself. Did you get sucked in?

Note: "Bugger", The Utility Word
The Australian language is constructed around utility words like "bugger" and "bastard" that have long lost their offensive nature. They express negatives in a number of different ways and reduce the need for an extensive and complicated vocabulary. Some examples are given below:

go to buggery
a means of letting someone know you no longer care for their future well-being or continuing presence
all to buggery
badly messed up
to play silly buggers
to waste time or badly mismanage a situation
to buggerise around
same as above
I'm buggered if I know
I'm stuck for a solution/I haven't a clue

"Bugger" is the Clayton's word of the Australian language. It's the word you have when you don't have the right word.

The Shortened Form

Australians are Aussies, bricklayers are brickies, biscuits are bikkies — it has never been satisfactorily explained why Australians are so fond of putting "ie" on the ends of words and virtually converting their language into baby talk, but the fact remains that a large part of the working vocabulary of the Australian language has been abbreviated to form shortened words that are now structures in their own right.

You get pressies at Chrissie. You go to the greengrocers for vegies, you take the kids to kindie, and if you're a tart you wear lippie. On summer evenings you get bitten by mozzies. If you're old and feeble you're a gerrie, and you probably wear a singie under your nightie, and a cardie as well. The slot machines are pokies, the fungi that grow in damp fields are mushies, and flat-soled shoes are flatties.

If an "ie" ending doesn't seem appropriate for the shortened form of a word, then an "o" is added instead.

Let me give you a œmo. Suppose you want some info on the lingo. I say it could take me all arvo. So instead I write you a memo and let you have a dekko. Good-oh.

If you have an oil fire you buy kero for it. When you're off working you might be doing a bit of bizzo, unless you're in the army when you're doing nashos. The one "o" you really must avoid is gastro.

Other common shortened forms to watch out for: a kangaroo is always a roo; if you go to university you're at uni, and the corner store is the deli. And Australia itself is Oz.

4

Compo

Mr Foster is on compo. He claims he did his back in. Actually he's just having a bit of a bludge. His mate Davo is a brickie. It's Thursdy arvo and they are building a barbie in the back yard. Mr Foster is unloading bricks off the back of Davo's ute when he sees a man in a grey suit.

Instant Conversation

MAN IN GREY SUIT:	I'm lookin for a Mr Foster.
LES:	E's not in.
DAVO:	Oo's this joker, Les?
LES:	God Botherer by the looks of it.
MAN IN GREY SUIT:	I'm from the insurance company. I'm lookin into a worker's compensation claim.
LES:	Aaaagh!

(Les collapses in a screaming heap on the pavement.)

DAVO:	You orright, Les?
LES:	Me back! It's gone again!
MAN IN GREY SUIT:	Wodyer think this is — Bush Week?
LES:	Holy shit. I'm in strife now.

21

MAN IN GREY SUIT:	Yer not wrong.
DAVO:	Yer nogunna dob im in?
MAN IN GREY SUIT:	Too right I am. E can't rip off the insurance office. That's just not on.
DAVO:	Miserable bastard!

Davo ups and jobs the man in the grey suit.

Vocabulary

compo
worker's compensation. Someone who uses worker's compensation as an habitual means of support is known as a "compo king"
to do one's back in
to have a back injury
having a bit of a bludge
taking advantage of the generosity of the welfare state or the trusting nature of an employer
brickie
bricklayer
barbie
a barbecue. Brick construction with a fireplace underneath and a hotplate on top, used for cooking sausages and steaks. The "backyard barbie" is a great Australian tradition. It has nothing whatever to do with nutrition (See also Lesson 10.)
backyard
back garden
ute
utility. A van with a tray top
joker
any stranger
God Botherer
One who touts religion. Australian God Botherers include Jehovah's Witnesses, Mormons and re-born Christians. Orange People (Neeshies) and devotees of Krsna are not included in this category, possibly because the God they bother is not immediately recognised as familiar

me* back
my back
wodyer think this is—Bush Week?
(now becoming less popular) exclamation of contempt used
to counter a tall story or when someone is trying to dupe you
in strife
in big trouble
yer not wrong
you're absolutely correct (Also "spot on".)
yer nogunna†
you're not going to
to dob in
to reveal someone's ruse to the relevant authorities
too right
certainly. Used to add emphasis to an expressed intention
to rip off
to extract money by fraudulent means. Can also mean to ask
for extortionate amounts of money for a product or service,
or to steal
not on
it cannot be allowed
bastard
in this context not a term of friendly familiarity
to up and job someone
to assault someone with the fists

---

*Possessive Pronouns
The Australian first person possessive pronoun is "me". The other
pronouns are:

yer — your	ow — our
is — his	yer — your
er — her	their — their

†Future Tense
You form the future tense in Australian by using the word "gunna",
prefixed with the appropriate present tense of the verb "to be".
Hence:

I'm gunna	We're gunna
Yer gunna	Yer gunna
E's gunna	They're gunna

23

Exercises

1. Pretend to do your back in. Claim compo. Did you get away with it for a period of six weeks or more? If yes, miss the next section and go on to page 27.
2. What do you think of Mr Foster's moral fibre? State your answer in less than five words.
3. Explain the word "compo" in your own words. Do not use the words "bludge", "rip off" or "government".
4. Write an essay on the Australian attitude to the work ethic.

What Do You Do for a Crust?

Everyone needs moolah. If you haven't got The Necessary they repo your wheels and turf you out of your fibro. So everyone needs a lurk. It's what you do for a crust.

A muso plays gigs and mainlines.

A pig is one of the boys in blue and busts you for speeding.

A quack gives you jabs and sees you right if you've got a wog.

A postie delivers letters.

A cockie lives out in the bush and whinges about the weather and the guvmint. (English migrants are renowned whinge-ers but farmers are a close second.)

A fruitologist sells vegies.

A medico does ops.

A wino or dero drinks plonk up the Cross. (Kings Cross. The area of Sydney around Darlinghurst Road — an uneasy alliance between Thomas Cook and dire straits.)

A milko delivers milk.

A journo writes for a rag and is always suspected of being a pinko or a commie.

A crim gives backhanders to the pollies (politicians) and knocks blokes off.

A bottle-o is a marine collector.

A legal eagle is someone you go to if you cop a bluey.

A narc busts you for smoking grass.

A spook wears dark glasses and a trenchcoat and works for ASIO (like the CIA but apparently totally incompetent; in Melbourne's Sheraton Hotel they are known as room service).

$\overrightarrow{L5}$

The Family Meal

It's teatime. Mrs Foster is in the kitchen. Shane is in the brasco, choking a darkie. Mr Foster is at the table, slinging off about the choongs and the pongos. Darlene is sitting next to him, quietly. She's just discovered she's up the duff.

Instant Conversation

LES: Wossfer tea? I could eat an orse an chase the jockey.

MAUREEN: Spag bog.

LES: Jeez, not ding food again. Woss wrong with chook?

MAUREEN: Had chook larse night. You doan like it, there's Vegemite inner cupboard. Make yerself a sammie.

(Les points at Darlene.)

LES: Woss *er* problem? Got a face like a wet week.

MAUREEN: Ardunno. Asker.

DARLENE: I think I'm pregnant.

(There is a long silence, known in Australia as the pregnant pause.)

LES: Oo is it? I'll go the bastard. Not that no-woper you brought rownere larse week?

DARLENE: Doan do yer block. It were nim.

LES: Oo was it then?

DARLENE: Ardunno. It was dark.

Les gives her a right-hander. Maureen picks up the jaffle-iron and drops him. Then it's on for young and old and Shane ends up calling the cops.

Vocabulary

brasco
lavatory. This word has fallen out of favour but is still sometimes heard. "Dunny" is still popular and in polite society it's called a "toot" (pronounced as in "soot")

to choke a darkie
to defecate. If you defecate in the open air you are said to "hit a blackfellow on the head". *Note*: These expressions have racist connotations and most people will be offended by them

to sling off
to make uncomplimentary remarks

choongs
the Chinese (Also "chinks".)

pongos
those of British extraction. This word is slowly replacing "pommies"

up the duff
pregnant (Also sometimes "preggers" or "preggo".)

I could eat an orse an chase the jockey
an expression used to denote great hunger (Also "me stomach thinks me throat's been cut" or "I could eat the crutch out of a low-flying duck" or "I could eat a baby's bum through a cane chair".)

spag bog
spaghetti bolognaise

ding
Italian

chook
chicken

Vegemite
black paste reputedly made from dead wombats and liquid

bitumen. Extremely popular in Australia, often served on toast for breakfast or on white bread for lunch or tea. Favoured to replace the kangaroo and the emu on the national emblem

sammie
sandwich

woss er problem?
what is ailing our delightful daughter?

to have a face like a wet week
to look miserable

Ardunno
I have no idea

I'll go the bastard
I will give the person responsible a severe physical beating

no-woper
a person with a restricted financial future and limited intellectual powers

rownere
this place. Corresponds to the French "chez nous"

to do one's block
to get extremely angry

to give someone a right-hander
to strike someone with the open hand (One can use either hand.)

jaffle-iron
heavy metal implement used for cooking toasted sandwiches

to drop someone
to strike someone with the open hand (one can use either hand)

it was on for young and old
a full-scale battle ensued

Exercises

1. Sling off about the choongs and the pongos in no less than fifty words. What should be done about them?
2. Do you think Mr Foster was justified in giving his daughter a right-hander? (a) Yairs (b) Nar (c) Ardunno.
3. Make up a sentence using the words "Vegemite", "jaffle-iron" and "brasco".
4. Do your block in Australian. (Time allowed: 2 minutes.)

Down the Beach

Tarts go down the beach to sunbake, and at beaches like Tamarama (sometimes called Glamarama because of the quality of the female flesh on display) and Bondi they just have sort of G-strings covering their pubes. Blokes go down the beach to perve at the talent. This is normally a furtive affair, unless three or more blokes are involved, in which case checking out the tarts can be a very noisy occupation.

Surfies go down the beach to catch waves and get wiped out. At Bondi the icebergs go in summer or winter.

Some beaches have sharkmesh between the heads but on other beaches the surfguard keeps a watch for the Noahs, from the safety of the surf club.

People are supposed to swim between the flags, where it's safe, but some joker always gets in strife, then the lifesavers have to go in to save him, and sometimes they have to get the Westpac chopper out for aerial rescues. If the surf gets too rough, the beach inspectors close the beach.

Some blokes like bodysurfing, but in a big surf you have to watch out for dumpers, and rips. If you get caught in a bad rip you could end up shark bait. Also, the bluebottles can be a right bastard in summer. These jellyfish give a very painful sting, but are preferable to sea-wasps or blue-ringed octopuses, which give a very painful death. If you get stung by one of them, you'll have carked it within minutes.

Most people go down the beach in bathers and sunnies. They used to wear cossies and some people still call them togs.

At dawn you always find the grommets down there trying to get in a couple of hours before school.

At night, the bogs get down the car parks next to the beach, and use them as drag strips to race their hot rods. They all have dirty great fats on the back and are mint for doing wheelies. The bogs also have gang bangs in the backs of the bog wagons and the last one in stirs the porridge.

16

In the Fish and Chippie

(New practitioners of Australian are often bemused by the accents they encounter when meeting Australians of southern European origin. The Greek and Italian migrants all speak a form of Australian we shall call Mediterstrinean.)

It is Fridy night. The stove is on the bung so Shane has volunteered to go down Nick's Fish and Chippie to get tea. The shop is owned by Nick Popodopopopolous who is as mad as a meat axe. Shane hopes to see Nick's daughter Maria, who is a top sort. Shane is not in the race, but is too much of a dill to realise this.

Instant Conversation

NICK: Yes mite.

SHANE: Four flake an eighty of chips. An two Chiko Rolls.

NICK: (calling) Maria! We needa more flike!

(Nick puts the chips in the fryer. He splashes himself with hot fat.)

NICK: Ow! Bloody thing!

(He goes out. Shane is left in the shop with Maria.)

SHANE: G'day.

(Maria smiles and says nothing.)

SHANE: I'm Shane. I live downer road. Hey er . . . feel like comin to the drives tomorra night?

(Maria giggles and blushes. Nick comes back.)

NICK: Maria! (to Shane) You toucha ma Maria, I brike you fice.

SHANE: Well jeez . . . orright then. Up you for the rent!

(Shane walks out.)

NICK: (to his wife, in Greek) Bloody foreigners!

Vocabulary

on the bung
not operational
fish and chippie
fish and chip shop
not in the race
without hope of success. One is also said to have "no show"
dill
an idiot
mite
mate. In Mediterstrinean all "ay" sounds are pronounced "i" with an accompanying nasal whine
flake
shark meat. Also known as "snapper", "dhufish" or even "cobbler", depending on which fish and chip shop you go to
Chiko Roll
(pronounced "chee-ko") a popular Australian fast food. Has similarities to the Chinese spring roll. Libel laws prevent me from saying where this similarity ends
bloody thing
the Mediterstrineans do not swear to the same extent as the ocker Australian, except in their mother tongue; "bloody thing" is an all-encompassing oath
the drives
the drive-in theatre. (Also known as "the passion pit".) The rear sections of drive-ins are renowned for steamed windows and grinding axlesprings

brike you fice
(literally "break your face") a threat of extreme physical violence
up you for the rent
(approximately) I no longer care to patronise you or any of your business interests

Exercises

1. What do you think of Shane's approach to Maria? Make up your own in less than 30 words. Do not use the word "drives".
2. Buy a Chiko Roll. Examine it closely. Can you think of an alternative use for it?
3. Do you think Nick was too hard on Shane or should he have simply stuck Shane's head in the hot fat? Answer yes or no.
4. Do you like Greeks? (a) Yairs (b) Nar. If you answered (b), on no account settle in Melbourne, which is the second largest Greek city in the world. (They probably won't like you either.)

Standard Responses

There are several questions and responses in the Australian language that should be learned by heart. The first is the characteristic Australian greeting:

"G'day, mate, owyagowin?"

The standard response to this is:

"Nobbad. Owsyerself?"

An alternative response is:

"Carn complain."

Among single Australian males the facetious "Gettin any lately?" should correctly be responded to with:

"Yeah, hadda putta man on."

If you get a job as a motor mechanic or land a position with the Public Service you must learn to practise "Ardunno". This is the correct response to any question or request for further information and should be repeated as often as necessary.

If anyone does a job well, or performs a service or favour for you, you say:

"Good on yer, mate."

If something is okay, you say:

"She's sweet" or (now less common) "She's apples".

The other standard responses that are absolutely imperative for anyone wishing to master basic Australian are "She'll be right" and "No worries" (known in some impolite circles as "no wuckin furries"). These words are uttered as a Pavlovian response to any request for assurance or more detailed information. They end any conversation and must be uttered while walking away with one hand waving nonchalantly in the air.

7

Getting a Job

Mr Foster has got the arse from his job. Davo tells him to come with him and see his foreman, as they're a bit light on at work. He says to come down straight away and be first cab off the rank.

Instant Conversation

(Early morning, the building site.)

DAVO: Remember — doan go off arf-cocked like yer always do. E's a bit niggly inner mornins.

(The foreman appears. He's built like a brick shithouse.)

FOREMAN: Oo's this peanut? Not another blow-in?

DAVO: It's the mate I told yer about. I need another offsider.

FOREMAN: Not a choom, izzy?

DAVO: No, no. E's dinky-di.

FOREMAN: Long as e's not like that larse useless bastard. Went walkabout after two days. Better be up to it . . . (to Les) . . . it's ard yakka, ya know.

DAVO: E'll keep is end up.

FOREMAN: Long as the two of youse doan stan roun

yabberin all day. E can front up Mundy, firs thing.

DAVO: Oh, ripper.

(The foreman walks off.)

DAVO: See. I said yer'd be sweet.

LES: Cheeky bastard. Lucky I dint drop im.

DAVO: Yairs, lucky orright. For you!

Vocabulary

to get the arse
to get the sack. In personal relationships one gets the elbow or the Big E
light on
short of manpower
first cab off the rank
first there. Usually implies getting in on an opportunity before anyone else
to go off half-cocked
to express opinions without first establishing the facts
niggly
irritable
built like a brick shithouse
of strong and sturdy physical build
peanut
an idiot
blow-in
a newcomer
offsider
a personal assistant, or number two
choom
an English person. Chooms are unwelcome in certain industries as they have a reputation for being habitual malcontents
to go walkabout
to disappear (From the Aboriginal habit of going off into the desert on a whim for weeks on end.)

ard yakka
hard work. Blokes who are willing to do some hard yakka
are about as scarce as rocking horse manure
to keep one's end up
to pull one's weight
youse
(pronounced "yews") the plural of "you"
to yabber
to chatter
to front up
to appear

Exercises

1. What do you think of chooms? Go off half-cocked in
   Australian.
2. What do you think of the foreman? Is he really a decent
   sort of joker deep down? (a) Yairs (b) Nar.
3. If you answered (a) go back to Lesson 1.

Geography and Politics

The Australian populace is divided into four distinct groupings: eastern staters (those from New South Wales and Victoria), banana benders (Queenslanders), crow eaters (South Australians) and gropers or sandgropers (Western Australians).

There are two other sub-groups which are the "daft inbred bastards" from Tassie (Tasmanians, also known as Taswegians) and the dying breed of drovers and stockmen from The Top End (Northern Territory).

The capital of Australia depends on where you live. Canberra is the official capital, Sydney thinks *it* is and Melbourne thinks *it* should be. Brissie (Brisbane) has no wish to be the capital of Australia — it's the capital of a separate nation, called Queensland.

Anyone who lives in Sydney will tell you what a soulless place Melbourne is, and in Melbourne they say the same thing about Sydney. Both opinions are correct.

If you live in a rural area you are a cockie or a bushie or a hick, and if you live in an urban area you are a city slicker. Sydney is The Big Smoke. Anywhere a thousand miles any side of The Alice (Alice Springs) is the Red Centre and is also the Back of Bourke and Beyond the Black Stump.

If you move to the country you've gone bush, and if you go to another country you're O.S. unless you're in England when you're in Pommyland.

In the cities, people are concerned about the Aboriginal problem, but in the outback they are more worried about the boongs and what to do with them.

Political opinion is strongly influenced by geography. The closer to the centre of the city, the further to the left you are. The reverse is also true. You therefore find the left-wing radicals in Darlinghurst and Glebe and the neo-fascists in outlying areas of Queensland and Western Australia.

In Canberra you find the Fat Cats (public servants living high off the profits of the tax system). These people have no political views since they retain government no matter who is in power.

8

Smoke-oh

Darlene is nine months gone, and Mr Foster is spewing about it. He's really dirty on her for getting preggers and all his mates are ragging him about it. Meanwhile Shane has got himself a cushie job in an office somewhere and reckons he's shit-hot.

Mr Foster is working with Davo. It is smoke-oh and they are sitting down having a brew. Mr Foster reckons it's a top lurk, as he's working fifty feet down and getting height allowance.

Instant Conversation

DAVO: Darlene dropped the kid yet?

LES: Any day now. She's too young dava bub. Should've adder boiler scraped when she adder chance.

DAVO: She'll be right. Ow's Shane? Eary landed onnis feet with this new job.

LES: In with some arty farty advertisin mob. E's only a gopher, but.

DAVO: Still. Better than a poke in the eye with a burnt stick, eh? Owdy jag that?

LES: Buggered if I know. Still, e ain't bludgin off me any more. Sharin a flat in Paddo with wunnervis mates.

44

DAVO: Paddo? Better watch it — doan wannim turnin inter an orse's oof.

(The siren goes.)

LES: Jees, orready? This is ard yakka. Think I'll ava sickie tomorra.

DAVO: Ripper idea. Get some tickets for the one-dayer, eh?

Vocabulary

spewing
very upset
to be dirty on
to be very angry with
to rag
to tease unmercifully
cushie
easy. Most cushie jobs are to be found in the Public Service
shit-hot
extremely clever
smoke-oh
a short rest during which workers are allowed to have a smoke and a cup of tea. The frequency and duration of smoke-oh depends on whether you are working for yourself or someone else. Cigarettes are "ciggies", "gaspers" or "cancer sticks"
brew
a cup of tea
top lurk
a well-paid and relatively easy job
height allowance
builders engaged in the construction of any edifice eight storeys or taller are allowed a height allowance under the union award, regardless of which storey they are working on. Consequently workers laying the foundations for an underground car park frequently receive a height allowance
to drop the kid
to give birth
dava
to have a

bub
baby
to have the boiler scraped
(crude vernacular) to have an abortion
eary
it has come to my attention that he
to land on one's feet
to receive a lucky break after a period of uncertainty
arty farty
having pretensions to artistic or aesthetic merit. Can be
applied to anything from the Sydney Opera House to a
kindergarten art teacher
gopher
a person who goes for things, i.e. a messenger (Also
"shitkicker".)
but
however. In correct Australian, it always appears at the end
of a sentence
better than a poke in the eye with a burnt stick
better than nothing
to jag
to procure by fortunate means
Paddo
Paddington. One-time working class suburb of Sydney, now
home to yuppies and gays
wunnervis
one of his
orse's oof
a homosexual (Popular rhyming slang: horse's hoof = poof.)
(Also "poofter".)
sickie
a day's paid leave due to sickness. In Australia it more often
means a day's paid leave under the guise of sickness
ripper
great. Australian adjective used universally for anything that
is considered very good (From "ripsnorter".)

Exercises

1. Should Darlene have had her boiler scraped? Offer moral and philosophical arguments in basic Australian. ("Buggered if I know" is not an acceptable answer.)
2. Name five things that are better than a poke in the eye with a burnt stick.
3. Use the word "ripper" in its proper context as many times as possible in the next 24 hours. (Minimum allowed: 50.)
4. Is your job ard yakka? Take a sickie.
5. Explain "arty farty" in your own words. (References to the Australian Literature Board inadmissible.)

Pubs

The staple of the Australian diet is piss, or to be more polite, grog. The average Australian likes nothing better than to "grog on" with his mates. This usually happens down the pub after work, or on a Sundy arvo from 4 to 7. This period is known reverently as The Session.

The choice of drinking receptacles is huge. The bottle shop — the licensed liquor outlet — sells stubbies, cans, bottles or tinnies, and in the bar of your pub or club you can buy your favourite amber fluid in a number of different-sized glasses.

Now at this point you will have to pay attention.

There are middies, schooners, glasses, pots, ponies, small beers, Hedland ponies, beer sixes, sevens, butchers, eights, handles, kites and pints.

A schooner's a 425 ml glass in New South Wales, but only a 285 mls in South Australia where a NSW schooner's a kite. A pot is 285 mls in Victoria and Queensland, but it's a middy in New South Wales and Western Australia, where a pot's 575 mls. (In New South Wales that's a pint.) A glass is 200 mls, except in Queensland where it's 225 mls and South Australia where it's a butcher and Northern Territory and New South Wales where it's a seven.

In Tasmania a small beer is 115 mls, in Queensland it's 140 mls, and in Victoria it's 170 mls. Back in Tasmania 170 mls is a beer six.

After this it starts to get complex, and I don't want to confuse you so we'll leave it there.

Anyone who spends a lot of time on the grog is a piss artist and if they get drunk very quickly they're a two-pot screamer. This term is usually applied to females and these types are very popular as they're cheap to take out.

These days someone is usually the skipper — often it's "the missus", sitting in the corner with her bitter lemon — so that the drinkers don't get done for DD.

Now, the level of alcohol in the blood that constitutes "drunk driving" is different from state to state and . . . sorry, did you say something?

9

At the Cricket

Mr Foster puts on his stubbies and heads off to the SCG for the cricket. He has arranged to meet Davo. Davo's brought his Esky, with two bottles of Coke and half a bottle of Bundy in each. They've come to watch the Windies do over the Aussies in the one-dayer.

Instant Conversation

LES: Strewth, that the score?

DAVO: Yeah, we're gettin creamed.

LES: Oo's on strike?

DAVO: Yewsie.

LES: That bastard's not worth feedin. Jeez, look at that — he shoulda oiked that over the fence. (shouts) Avago ya mug!

DAVO: Givim a go. E nearly wore that roun the ear.

LES: Eh, there's a big blue started on the Ill. Least we'll see some action — this is a right fizzogg.

(Later.)

DAVO: Reckon the Windies are omen osed.

LES: Yeah, we got Buckley's. Wanna shoot through?

DAVO: No way. I'm stayin to the death. I'm gettin me

seven bucks worth outta Kerry Packer. Richards'll start ittin sixes in a mo, no worries.

LES: Hoggie's really takin some stick.

DAVO: Yeah — dropped is bundle after Richards it that last bandry. Reckon eorta give it away.

LES: Wanna dog's eye?

DAVO: Yeah, orright. Eh — an remember the tom sauce this time.

LES: Orright, save me pozzie.

(There is a wild yell from the crowd.)

DAVO: Eh Les — watch yerself!

(There is a sickening thud and a groan.)

DAVO: Poor bastard. Toldim Richards'd start ittin sixes soon . . .

Vocabulary

stubbies
Australian shorts. Black, worn just below the beergut and gathered nattily around the crutch. These are required dress for the cricket, and are worn in conjunction with a beer-stained T-shirt

beergut
Australian national costume

Esky
an insulated drink cooler. Packed with ice it will keep drinks cold for anything up to half an hour on a really hot day

Bundy
Bundaberg rum (Bundaberg is a sugar-growing town in Queensland.)

Windies
the West Indies cricket team

one-dayer
one-day cricket international

strewth
once common ocker oath, now heard much less frequently

creamed
annihilated
Yewsie
Kim Hughes, one-time Australian cricket captain. The greatest honour bestowed on Australia's favourite sporting sons is having "ie" tacked onto the end of their names, as in Marshie, Woodie, Hoggie and, of course, Dougie. Lillee was born to greatness, having had the "ie" sound thoughtfully attached to his surname at birth
not worth feedin
of inferior talent or ability
to oick
to hit something into the air with great force
avago ya mug
almost literally, "Don't just stand there you fool, do something"
givim a go
give that person a fair chance
to wear
to be on the receiving end of
blue
a fight. If the fight takes place in a pub, it's sometimes called a "donnybrook" or a "stoush"
the Ill
the Hill — the grassed area of the Sydney Cricket Ground without seats; the cheapest area of the ground with a reputation for blues, banners, buglers, barrackers and boozers
fizzogg
a disappointingly uncompetitive game (Also "fizzer".)
omen osed
(literally "home and hosed") winning by such a margin that the rest of the game has become a formality
Buckley's
if you have Buckley's chance, you have no chance whatsoever (Also heard as: "You've got two chances — none and Buckley's." Said to have derived from the Melbourne department store, "Buckley's and Nunn".)
to shoot through
to leave (From the saying: "Shoot through like a Bondi tram", meaning to depart with great haste.)

to the death
till the end of the game
in a mo
short for "in a moment"
to take stick
to take a beating verbally or in terms of competition
eorta
he ought to
to give it away
to give up or retire
dog's eye
a meat pie; a soggy pastry case containing gravy, blood clots and elastoplast. Popular at sports grounds and lunch bars
tom sauce
tomato ketchup. Popular in Australia because of its ability to mask the flavour of meat pies
pozzie
position or seat

Exercises

1. Describe the recent performances of the Australians against the West Indies using the words "not worth feedin", "Buckley's" and "give it away".
2. Buy a meat pie. Eat it. Keep it down for half an hour. Did you enjoy the taste? If so, move to the end of the book and graduate with honours.

Common Causes of Mistakes

There are certain words in the Australian vocabulary that can cause a great deal of confusion and embarrassment to people unfamiliar with the language, and we'll go through the most important of them here.

First of all, if an Australian asks you for durex, he is not requesting a loan of a condom. He wants some sticky tape (known in England as Sellotape). On the other hand, if he asks you for a rubber, you'll have to decide whether he wants an eraser or something else entirely. If the latter, tell him to get nicked and get his own from the machine in the men's dunny.

When you go to watch the cricket, or the football, you don't root for your team. You barrack. If you want to root, you stay home and do it in private.

Americans sit on their fannies. Australians sit on their bums, or if they're public servants, their fat arses. Only Australian girls have fannies, and they don't sit on them, unless they're riding a horse.

A crook is a crim. If you're crook, you take a sickie, and if you're *really* crook you go to the quack and claim compo.

If you are a negro and an Australian asks someone to cut him a slice of coon, don't get offended. In Australia Coon is a sort of cheese.

Knockers are complainers, so if you hear someone say they're sick and tired of knockers, they are not revealing their sexual preferences. In

Australia knockers are generally boobs or norks. Or titties. Also, if your secretary claims she's not getting a decent screw, it is not necessarily an invitation. She could mean you're not paying her enough.

Two other points to remember: you will give yourself away as a foreigner, even if you master every other point in this book, if you pronounce "scone" as in "bone". The correct pronunciation is "skon".

Finally, in Australia an Alsatian dog is a German Shepherd. (It is necessary to absorb this fact in order to understand the popular Australian joke: "What's black and brown and looks good on an advertising account executive? A German Shepherd.")

Ĺ1 L̈0

Going on a Barbie

Mrs Foster has organised with Davo's wife Shirl for them all to go for a barbie in the Ku-ring-gai. It's freezing, so they get rugged up and hit the road. Mr Foster reckons he'd rather spend the weekends at home than tear-arsing around the countryside.

Davo brings his daughter Leigh, her boyfriend, a drongo called Jason, and their two ankle-biters. As soon as they get there Davo and Mr Foster crack the tinnies, while Mrs Foster and Shirl sit down and start flapping their gums, and Jason is left in charge of cooking the snaggers.

Instant Conversation

DAVO: Check it out — coulden organise a piss-up in a brewery. Ace it up son — yer burnin the snags!

JASON: Doan go crook at me! You cook the bastards!

(He stomps off. There is a scream.)

DAVO: Wossgowinon?

SHIRL: Little Darryl lost is thong an there's bindis right through the grass.

DAVO: I told imter wear sanshoes! Little sook — tell imter stop blubbin or e'll get a right-ander.

(There is another scream — shriller than the first.)

DAVO:	Now what?
LEIGH:	Desiree's got bombed by the maggies.
SHIRL:	No bloody wonder. She was firin er ging attem.
LEIGH:	She's bleedin. Anyone got a Band-aid?

(The blowies appear out of nowhere. Desiree chucks up over Davo's trousers. Les decides to nick off. He gets in the Kingswood, chucks a u-ey and heads back towards the main drag.)

DAVO:	Wairyagowin? We was jus startin dava good time! (to the others) Jeez . . . owd ya be, eh?

Vocabulary

barbie
a barbecue. This is *the* great Australian institution, the holy of holies. Prerequisites are sausages, rancid margarine, a few steaks the texture and size of doormats, and a picnic spot with hot plates, green branches, bull ants and a chapter of the local Hell's Angels. The rest of the ritual will be explained below
freezing
any temperature below 25°C
rugged up
dressed up in warm clothes
to tear-arse
to rush around
drongo
one not endowed with great mental resources, usually having lank hair and a vacant expression
ankle-biters
small, noisy, unruly children; or any children
to crack the tinnies
to open cans of beer
to flap the gums
to talk incessantly and rapidly; to gossip
snagger
a sausage (Also "snag".) Australian sausages are traditionally

thin, pink, obscene and tasteless. They are used as a medium for eating tom sauce

check it out
look at that

couldn't organise a piss-up in a brewery
useless

ace it up
a request to improve one's performance

doan go crook at me
don't get upset with me

wossgowinon?
a form of general enquiry

thong
a sort of rubber sandal (Known in England as a flip flop.)

bindi
a grass thorn that follows unsuspecting Australians through the grass, waiting for them to remove their shoes (Also "bindi-i".)

sanshoes
(literally "sandshoes") canvas footwear (In England they are known as plimsolls.)

sook
(pronounced as in "look") a crybaby

to blub
to cry

maggies
magpies (Sometimes known as "black and white ducks".) In spring they intimidate and sometimes attack schoolchildren with low dives in order to protect their nests

ging
a child's catapult (Sometimes known as a "shanghai".)

blowies
blowflies. Another prerequisite of the Australian barbie. They always appear out of nowhere. It's traditional

to chuck up
to vomit

to nick off
to depart (Also "P.O.Q.", short for "piss off quick".)

to chuck a u-ey
to make a u-turn

main drag
main road
wairyagowin?
where are you off to?
we was*
past tense of "we are"
owd ya be?
has no meaning. A general expression of disgust or wonderment

Exercises

1. Put some toothpaste in a frying pan. Cook it. Drop it on the floor. Eat it. This is the taste and consistency expected from a barbied snagger.
2. Practise bringing your child up in the Australian manner: tell it not to be a sook; order it to stop blubbing; give it a right-hander. (Not necessarily in that order.)
3. Put your finger down your throat. Chuck up.
4. Explain in your own words why Desiree is a stupid name to give a child, especially an Australian girl.
5. Organise a piss-up in a brewery.

*****Was**
The past tense of the verb "to be" is "was", which is easy to remember, i.e.:

I was	we was
you was	you was
he/she/it was	they was

Sport

Cricket is the national summer sport but winter sports are more diverse. In Queensland and New South Wales they play Rugby League and Rugby Union. In South Australia, Western Australia (Dubble Yeway), Tassie and Vic they play footie. In the Northern Territory they play with their puds.

Footie — or Australian Rules Football — is a man's game, and there's no place in it for creampuffs. Players frequently go the bash, and so sometimes one of them ends up a cot case. When that happens, the bloke responsible cops a bluey from the umpire.

Even though it is a man's game, there's a surprising amount of concentration on behinds in every match — but players only get one point for a behind. They have to get it right through the middle for a goal, which is worth six points.

The game is played on an oval. When a player makes a good play, it's a ball tearer, unless he's one of the opposition, in which case it's pure arse. The game is either a bottler (if your team wins) or a fizzogg (if it doesn't). At the end of the season the winning team all get a gong each.

To barrack for your team you shout "Carn the Blues" or "Carn Swans" or whatever, unless you support St Kilda, in which case you don't say much at all, you just stand behind the goals and look miserable.

11 11
Buying a
Pre-loved Car

Shane goes with Macka to look at a set of wheels. Macka reckons he's got the clues and can pick a bodgie a mile off. The car is a red Charger with a white racing stripe, mag wheels, fats on the back and all the fruit.

Instant Conversation

SHANE: Wodya reckon? Mickey Mouse, eh?

MACKA: These things suck up the juice, mate. Ow much duzzy want?

SHANE: Three narf.

MACKA: Sounds a bit shonky ter me. Reckon emusta flogged it.

SHANE: It's in good nick. Check the duco. Six months reggo too.

MACKA: It's ad a re-spray. Reckon it's been in a prang.

(The owner emerges from the house.)

MACKA: This the joker? Looks like a rule lair ter me.

LAIR: G'day gents. Wanna take it roun the block?

(Macka and Shane get in. A few minutes later.)

SHANE: Well?

64

MACKA: It's cactus. Reckon it's been roun the clock a few times. Engine's clapped out, an it needs a new muffler.

SHANE: Yeah, but check the stereo, mate.

(He turns up the sound full blast.)

SHANE: Mint, eh?

(They get back to the lair's house. Shane gets out.)

SHANE: I'll take it.

MACKA: Jeez mate — yer got rocks in yer ed!

Vocabulary

pre-loved
used (Also "pre-owned".) In Australia pre-owned car salesmen sell pre-loved cars, and sometimes vice versa
got the clues
to have expert knowledge. Such a person may also be a "bit of a gun" or a "dead hand"
bodgie
something that is not all it seems. Not a quality product
fats
wide tyres
all the fruit
every known accessory, e.g. stereo, electrically operated aerial, interior light dimmer, and a doodewacker hanging from the rear vision mirror
doodewacker
a doovelacky
doovelacky
a gizmo
gizmo
a gadget which has no known appropriate name
Mickey Mouse
really good. Rhyming slang for "grouse", which these days is seldom heard
to suck up the juice
to consume large quantities of petrol. If a car is economical it "runs on the smell of an oily rag"

shonky
of dubious quality. In other words, "not fair dinkum"
to flog
to steal, but can also mean to sell
reggo
motor vehicle registration
in good nick
in good condition
duco
paintwork
prang
an accident
lair
a youth with hooligan qualities. Can also mean loud, as in tasteless, e.g. a lairish/lairy tie. Lairs generally cruise the high street on a Saturday night in their cars, whose radios are invariably twice as loud as their engines
cactus
of no further value
clapped out
worn out from overuse
muffler
a silencer
to have rocks in the head
to be unwise

Exercises

1. Put together an Australian sentence using the words "doovelacky", "doodewacker" and "gizmo".
2. Write an essay on why Shane has rocks in his head. Use both sides of the paper.
3. Think of a lair you know. Go round to his house and let down his tyres. Are you still in good nick?

Days, Dates, Weather, Time

Days and Dates

In Australian, the days of the week are: Mundy, Chewsdy, Wensdy, Thersdy, Fridy, Saddy, and Sundy.

The big days to remember during the year are Chrissie and Anzac Day. At Chrissie you get pressies and get pissed to the eyeballs. On Anzac Day the diggers all go on a march to the Memorial and everyone else has a day off and gets pissed to the eyeballs.

Weather

In Australia the weather varies little. Around most of the country it is either "pissing down" (Melbourne), "brass monkeys" (Canberra) or "bloodyot" (Perth). Emphasis is added with the prefix "Jeez":

"It's very hot" — "Jeez, it's frigginot today."

"It's very cold" — "Jeez, it's brass monkeys orright."

"It's raining/drizzling/coming down in torrents" — "Jeez, it's pissin down."

The only other type of weather occurs up in the northern tropical regions where there is occasionally a cyclone, known as a "blow", or a "big blow" if it wipes out the city. In the far north these often occur during the rainy season, or "Wet", between December and March.

Telling Time

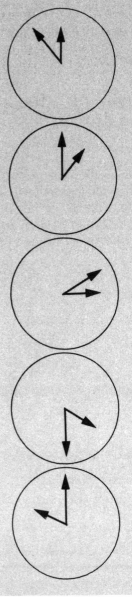

Feel like a liquid lunch today?

Better get back ter the office in a mo.

Ker-ist, look at the time!

Time for anotherie?

Better give the missus a bell, teller I'll be a bit late.

$\overset{\cdot}{L_1} \ \overset{\cdot\cdot}{L_2}$

Visiting the Family

Shane has decided to visit his oldies. He gets on the blower and tells them he's coming over Sundy. Mrs Foster reckons he's come good and makes a lammie, special. Mr Foster reckons he's up himself since he joined the ad agency but. He says all his mates are a bunch of would-be-if-they-could-be's. He intends to give him a serve.

Instant Conversation

(The Charger pulls up outside the Foster residence.)

LES: I dint know ewas lobbin sarvo.

MAUREEN: I told ya yesterdie.

LES: Wossat e's drivin? Musta knocked it off from somewhere.

SHANE: G'day.

LES: Where ja get that? Wodid that set ya back?

SHANE: We're not all on the bones of our arse.

LES: If that's paid for, I'll stand the season.

MAUREEN: Give it a break, Les. Lettim get inner door.

LES: E's flogged it. Sticks out like dog's balls. (sniffs) Jeez, somethin's on the nose.

SHANE: It's aftershave.

LES: Ker-ist. Ya smell like a Turkish brothel.

SHANE: I'm jacka this. Larse time I come rownere.

(Shane nicks off.)

LES: Typical. Bastard never comes to see us, anwenny does e only stays five minutes.

Vocabulary

oldies
parents

blower
the telephone. This is what you give people a bell on (Also the "gasser".)

to come good
to improve, after not initially reaching expectations. The Prodigal Son is a good example of someone who "came good"

lammie
lamington (See Basic Australian: Food.)

special
in this context "especially for the occasion"

to be up oneself
to be egotistically enamoured of oneself

would-be-if-they-could-be's
posers; people who consider they are better than others but do not have the status or the money to prove it

to give someone a serve
to give someone a piece of your mind

to lob
to arrive unexpectedly

sarvo
this afternoon

to knock off
to steal

wodid that set ya back?
how much did that cost you?

on the bones of one's arse
destitute

I'll stand the season
expression similar in intention to "I'm a monkey's uncle"

give it a break
let us not continue with this discussion
to stick out like dog's balls
to be quite obvious
on the nose
smelly
I'm jacka this
I'm tired of this. *Note*: In Australian the word "of" is rarely pronounced. Hence "I'm jack of this" becomes "I'm jacka this"
anwenny does
and then when he does

Exercises

1. Name one American President who has "come good". (Time limit: 30 minutes.)
2. Name one Australian Prime Minister who has "come good". (Time limit: 30 days.)
3. Get on the blower and give someone you're jack of a serve.

Food

The staple of the Irish diet is the potato. The staple of the Asian diet is rice. The staple of the Australian diet (after grog) is cholesterol.

Traditional Australian food (like campfire-baked damper and those cubes of stale sponge-cake coated in chocolate and coconut known as "lamingtons") has given way to the take-away invasion. Now gourmet cooking means anything outside the range of burgers, battered savs (deep-fried sausages in batter — inedible, but useful for oiling your bike), barbecued chooks, doner kebabs and pizzas with "furry fish". Some of this can be really crook food, but that doesn't stop a hearty Australian appetite.

Australians in general aren't bad on the tooth. Those in the bush like their tucker, but urban Australians just like a bloody good feed. They all love steaks (and still sometimes eat them with eggs for brekkie), but seafood is increasingly popular, especially crays, yabbies, snapper, jewy and bream. You might also hear of blokes having lamb's fry for breakfast, but this now means just liver and bacon, where once it was a polite expression for lamb's cods (or testicles).

The great Australian dessert is pavlova, which is made of all those ingredients necessary to bring on an immediate myocardial infarction.

After a good feed an Australian will tell you that it really hit the spot. It may not have even touched the sides.

Sometimes you will hear someone tell you they're having a show and they're putting a keg on and everyone's chucking in to pay for it. In this case the food will often be laid on by the host, but sometimes the ladies will all bog in to help prepare it.

If you dine out you'll look for somewhere to get some cheap eats. A lot of these places are B.Y.O., so you Bring Your Own grog, often in your own Esky, which gets pride of place in the centre of the dining table.

The kids like lollies, and they like them just as much if you call them sweets or candy instead, and will want you to buy them Freddo Frogs, Violet Crumble Bars and Jaffas. On special occasions they get fairy bread (sliced white bread topped with hundreds and thousands). Some kids will still ask for googies — boiled, fried or scrambled — for breakfast and occasionally you'll hear an adult call them bumnuts.

A "Lifesaver" can also be a sort of lolly, so if you hear your lady say she wants to suck on a lifesaver there is no need to be alarmed . . . unless you live near the beach.

There are few regional differences in cuisine, though the "floater" (a meat pie floating in thick pea soup) is found only in Adelaide, the city which, perhaps coincidentally, has the highest suicide rate in the country. But there do exist regional variations in terminology: thus the popular sausage made of meat-flavoured cereal which is known as "poloni" in Dubble Yeway, changes its name, though unfortunately not its taste, on its trip across the Nullarbor, to become "devon" in NSW.

13

In the Pub

Mr Foster knows he's alive. He's been busier than a brickie in Beirut. Fridy night, he and Davo go down the Tab. Davo has a dead cert for the trots. It runs like a hairy goat so they go down the rubbedy for a quick one to drown their sorrows.

Instant Conversation

LES: What appened to the dead cert, ya galah?

DAVO: Doan get snakey with me. Thought I was doin the right thing.

LES: Oh yeah. I'm right in the noo-er when the missus fines out. Ain't got a cracker for the resta the week.

DAVO: Yer not Robinson Crusoe. Carn, doan perform. I'll shout yer a beer.

LES: Larse bleedin time I listen to you, fair dinkum.

DAVO: Ya know what they say: "Life wasn't menda be easy."

(The Lotto draw comes up on the box at the end of the bar. Les checks his coupon. He has five correct numbers. He is beside himself.)

DAVO: You arsey bastard. Yer gunna be quids in.

LES: Oh you little bewdy.

The Salvos come round with the tin. Les decides it's time to choof off.

Vocabulary

to know one is alive
to become aware that one was previously comparatively well off
busier than a brickie in Beirut
very busy. A more common form is "flat out like a lizard drinking" or just "flat chat"
the Tab
the Totalisator Agency Board (government-controlled betting offices)
dead cert
a sure thing
to run like a hairy goat
to perform poorly on the racetrack
rubbedy
a pub (Rhyming slang: rubbedy dub = pub.) A term no longer in common use but occasionally heard. To Australians the pub is an all-encompassing expression taking in both the local licensed drinking house and the five-star Regent Hotel in Sydney, currently Australia's premier "pub"
a quick one
a drink. Anything from one round to a longer session where one is reported missing in the newspapers
galah
a derogatory term. A galah is a native pink and grey parrot noted for its raucous cry while hanging upside down from telegraph wires
snakey
irritable
to do the right thing
to act in the correct manner
in the noo-er
(from "in the manure" or "in the shit") in trouble
the missus
my spouse. In correct Australian, the words "missus" and

"wife" are always preceded by "the", never by a possessive pronoun

not to have a cracker
to be without money (Also "without a brass razoo", pronounced "rah-zoo".)

you're not Robinson Crusoe
you're not the only one

carn
come on

don't perform
don't make a fuss

to shout a beer
to buy a beer (for someone else). Used as either a verb or a noun, "shout" is one of the most important words in the Australian language. Those visitors who haven't time to master the language as a whole will be well-received if they learn only the phrase "My shout", and use it as often as possible

fair dinkum
honest. Anything that is fair dinkum is inviolable truth. The phrase thus adds emphasis to any claim, promise or (often) threat

life wasn't meant to be easy
a phrase coined by a recent Australian PM, but we shall not name the phraser. The utterance became at once notorious, and has since slipped into common usage as a glib ripost in a number of different contexts. Basically though: "Hard luck"

to be beside oneself
to be extremely agitated

arsey bastard
a very fortunate person

quids in
prosperous

you little bewdy
an expression used to convey happiness

Salvos
Salvation Army personnel, frequently seen in the public bars of city pubs, soliciting donations. This works as a sort of alcoholics' super fund, as donors often end up as recipients 20 years and 50,000 more middies down the track

choof off
polite expression for "depart"

Exercises

1. Give three alternative Australian expressions meaning "choof off". Be vulgar. Extra marks will be awarded for obscenity.
2. Write an essay on going for a quick one and then getting in the noo-er with the missus.
3. Explain in your own words why life wasn't meant to be easy.

The Outback

The Outback is somewhere out the back of Bourke, near Woop Woop, and Bullamakanka, the other side of the rabbit proof fence. It consists of mallee, scrub and mulga; roos and gibber plains; ragged mountain ranges, droughts and flooding . . . Well, you get the picture.

The people who live out there are a minority cult group called dinkum Aussies. They are divided into cockies, drovers and jackaroos. Pastoralists and graziers are cockies. So are cattle barons. Drovers and jackaroos do all the work.

The outback is also the best place to find Aborigines. They live in humpies. For some reason, they are not included in the count of dinkum Aussies. Nor are miners (except tin-scratchers and opal-gougers). Nor are women of any description.

Outback wildlife consists of brumbies, dingoes, goannas, kookaburras, galahs, koalas, wombats and possums. The platypus is found mainly in zoos and on coins. The biggest hazards are crocs, willy-willies, and getting lost in the bush.

The focus of the country towns are the pubs. In this part of the country Slim Dusty is the musical equivalent of Bruce Springsteen and Joan Sutherland, all rolled in one.

Country pubs are still the place for a blue. You can still hear some bloke get accused of poddy-dodging and the accuser will be told to pull his head in. Before long someone else will stick their bib in, and before you know it some bloke decides to go the knuckle and gets done over.

The main function of the bush is to grow wheat, raise sheep and cattle and provide a gerrymander for right-wing politicians.

Mainly the latter.

$$L\dot{1}\;L\dot{4}$$

Going to a Show

Shane is sharing a terrace house with Aaron, another bloke who works for the arty farty advertising mob. A friend of Aaron's is having a show. Shane is really bunging on an act and sucking up to all the trendies. He's hanging out for his first root and has his eyes on a bushfire blonde in the corner.

Instant Conversation

SHANE: Top show. Real rage.

AARON: It's orright. Wodyer thinka the decor. Really kitsch, eh?

SHANE: Cop the tart over there with the red air. Top sort.

AARON: Wait'll she opens er mouth. Rough as guts. Anyway, the moll's on with some bloke oo runs a porno shop.

SHANE: Woss the mail on the joker with the leather pants? Looks like a bit of a bumjumper ter me.

AARON: Jeez, you're really passé sometimes Shane. Bein gay's all the go these days.

SHANE: I'll still keep me freckle to the wall, thanks.

AARON: Suit yerself. I'm gunna go over an ava mag with im. Is name's Enzo.

SHANE: Bloody dings.

84

AARON: E's stinkin. Drives a Roller.

SHANE: (interested) Zat right?

Shane and Aaron go over to Enzo and start pissing in his pocket. Shane gets absolutely full, tries to con up his boss's wife, and shits in his own nest.

Vocabulary

show
party

to bung on an act
to feign a personality superior to one's own

to suck up
to ingratiate oneself

trendies
lower class Beautiful People

to hang out for
to be in a state of fevered anticipation

bushfire blonde
(only occasionally heard) a redhead

rage
a good time, invariably involving drinking and often dancing as well

kitsch
vulgar or in poor taste (Also "tacky" or "off" or "rank".)

cop
word used to draw attention to something. Often heard as "cop this"

rough as guts
vulgar or uncouth (Also "rough as bags".)

moll
a tart with no class

to be on with
to be amorously involved with

to have the mail on
to have information about

bumjumper
a homosexual (Also "shirt-lifter" or "pillow-biter"; more commonly "queer" or "gay".)

passé
behind the times. Recent years have seen the emergence of a new Australian dialect, used solely by the trendies and their admirers. Known as "Nouveau Oz", it consists of jargon and bastardised French, larded onto Basic Australian. "Passé", pronounced preferably with a slight lisp, is a Nouveau Oz key-word. Other examples are "per se", "scenario", "situation", "holistic", "methodology", "feedback", "in respect of", "restrospective to" and . . . "workshop"

all the go
fashionable

freckle
anus (Sometimes "quoit" or "blurter".)

to have a mag with
to talk to

stinking
extremely rich. Such a person has "oodles" of dough

to piss in someone's pocket
to ingratiate oneself; to "suckhole"

full
extremely drunk

to shit in one's own nest
to earn a bad reputation for yourself in your own territory

Exercises

1. What hope has Shane got of becoming a trendie? Answer carefully in one word.
2. What do you think of Shane's new friend, Aaron? Be personal.
3. Get a mirror. Put it between your feet. Bend over. Locate your freckle.
4. Write an essay on contemporary Australian culture using the words "kitsch", "tacky" and "passé".

Having a Naughty

The act of sex has become entrenched in the language as "having a naughty". There are a number of ways you can have a naughty in Australia. If you do it in a phone box it's a knee trembler; before breakfast it's a morning glory. Some people even have a "winky pops". (The Winky Pops is the name of a small bay near Manly famous among surfies as a place for jumping on boards by day and on broads by night.)

You can also dip the wick, sink the sausage or have a nooky.

If this happens a lot you'll earn a reputation as a spunk bandit. Spunk bandits are always in like Flynn and never get a knock-back. They're always on a promise.

Intercourse in Australia consists of a bloke and a tart getting their gear off and jumping in the sack in the nuddy. The bloke is required to crack a fat, or crack a mongrel. Unless the tart is on the Pill, the bloke wears a frenchie or a franger on his old feller or pork sword; otherwise she could get up the duff. If the tart shows a certain enthusiasm for sexual activity, she's said to bang like a dunny door in a gale. But if she's not keen, it may be necessary for Mrs Palm and her five daughters to take matters in hand.

The warm, intimate moments after lovemaking are known in Australia as the Sunday Session. The warm, intimate moments before lovemaking, known in other countries as foreplay, do not exist in Australia.

L1 L5

Waking Up

Shane and Aaron have crashed at Aaron's mate's pad. Shane is not feeling too clever when he wakes up. He has a mouth like an abo's armpit. He stumbles out in his jocks. Aaron is having brekkie.

Instant Conversation

AARON: Cop the eyes on it. They're like pissholes in the snow.

SHANE: I musta knocked back a few.

AARON: Ya were paraletic. (offering him a glass of warm beer) Wanna heart starter?

SHANE: Jeez no. I'd heave.

AARON: Well ya better go an ava tub. We're meetin this joker at 10.

SHANE: What joker?

AARON: The bloke we said we'd do the job for. *You* know — Enzo. We gotta pick up a parcel from the airport for im.

SHANE: A parcel? That's a bit of a worry. We don't know the bloke from a bara soap.

AARON: Nothin to it. Miteswell give it a punt. We're both shorta the readies.

(Shane baulks at the idea. He doesn't want to be in it. He'd rather not have any truck with Enzo.)

SHANE: Wait on. E's not a crim, izzy?

AARON: Jeez, ya know me Shane. Would I give ya a bum steer?

SHANE: Ardunno. Think I'll take a rain check. Reckon e's a bit of a flake.

AARON: It's worth a coupla undred each.

SHANE: On the other and, e is a mate a yaws.

AARON: That's the shot.

Vocabulary

to crash
to bed down. Crashing is usually associated with reaching your limit of exhaustion and/or inebriation and being unable to get yourself home
not to feel too clever
to feel terrible
a mouth like an abo's armpit
a furry mouth after a heavy night's drinking. An "abo" is an Aborigine; the word is often construed as a derogatory term, but, given the Australian penchant for abbreviation, it probably wasn't meant to be. However, whites who don't want to be thought racist are careful not to use it
brekkie
breakfast
pissholes in the snow
common metaphor used to describe the optical condition brought on by drunkenness and late nights
to knock back a few
to imbibe large quantities of alcoholic liquor
paraletic
paralytic, meaning drunk. "Rotten" is another form
heart starter
the first alcoholic drink the morning after a heavy night's drinking. Supposed to have recuperative qualities

to heave
to vomit. There are numerous Australian words to describe this popular bodily function. "Chunder" is another of the more common ones
tub
a shower
a bit of a worry
something perturbing or suspect. A useful expression, covering a lot of territory; anything from the threat of nuclear annihilation to Molly Meldrum's taste in music can be a bit of a worry
we don't know the bloke from a bar of soap
that fellow is a complete stranger to us
give it a punt
give it a try (Also "give it a burl".)
short of the readies
short of money
to give a bum steer
to mislead
to take a rain check
to postpone indefinitely
flake
a person of suspect moral character (Also "shark" or "shyster".)
that's the shot
expression of approval similar to "that's the spirit"

Exercises

1. Is Shane about to get sucked in again? (a) Yairs (b) Nar.
2. If you answered (b) to question 1 go back to the beginning of the book and start again. You really must try harder.
3. Have you been to any top shows recently? Did you get paraletic? (a) Yairs (b) Nar.
4. If you answered (b) to question 3 go back to the first lesson with the other bloke and start again. And try to pay attention in future, both of you.

Australian Society

Australia is a classless society. However.

In this classless society there are three classes. Upper, middle and lower. Plus there are some people who live below the lower class, with no hope of rising higher. These include the deros of the inner urban areas and most of the abos, most of whom haven't got a skerrick, and spend most of what little they have on the terps getting rotten.

The lower class is generally the Ockers and they're mainly interested in going to the footy on a Saddy, then finishing up at the pub and getting rotten. The Ockers are worried that the slant-eyes, slopeheads, wogs and other reffos are going to take over the joint, but the middle class is more laid back about the ethnics and more concerned with lifestyle — which means going out three times a week for a good feed and getting rotten.

The gulf between the middle class and the upper class is filled by the Micks. In Sydney this group is known as the Catholic Mafia and most of them work for Auntie ABC. They have a lot of clout and get rotten in private clubs.

The big bikkies is divided into old money and new money. Possessors of both types drive Rollers. For recreation and culture they take their fifty foot Bertrands out on the river and get rotten.

The fair dinkum, dinki-di, true-blue Australians are mostly found in RSL clubs getting rotten. Most of them are over 65 and therefore out to grass. They often have dicky tickers. These die-hard conservatives want to keep the present flag and go back to "God Save the Queen" as the national anthem, but your average Joe Blow doesn't give a stuff about the flag or the Royals. He doesn't give a stuff about the present anthem, "Advance Australia Fair", either, and doesn't know the words.

Ĺ1 Ĺ6

Getting Busted

Shane and Aaron pick up the parcel at the airport, no worries. Shane is pretty toey about the whole bizzo. He is wearing his shades so no one will recognise him.

Instant Conversation

(In the airport carpark.)

AARON: Doan stan there like a stunned mullet. Get inner car.

SHANE: I doan wanna bara this. There could be arfa tunna smack in there.

AARON: Yer not gunna cop out now. Come on— we're late.

SHANE: What iffy *is* a crim?

AARON: Iffy is, we ain't got time to stan ere an argue the toss. Now stop fartarsin aroun an drive the car!

SHANE: Orright, doan get ostile!

AARON: (mutters) Pissweak!

(Later. At Enzo's house.)

ENZO: Ya getta the stuff off the pline?

AARON:	No worries. Earyah. Now then — what about our cop?
SHANE:	Talkina cops . . . wossat comin up the drive?
ENZO:	Bloody thing! We uppa shit crick boys!
POLICEMAN:	I'd like a look in that bag, thanks.
SHANE:	It's muesli.
POLICEMAN:	Turn it up. I dint come down inner larse share. Yer all busted.

Shane is off like a bride's nightie. One of the Ds rugby tackles him and he is dragged off down the cop shop.

Vocabulary

toey
nervous
bizzo
business
shades
sunglasses
like a stunned mullet
with an unintelligent expression on the face. Common usage
not to want a bar of
to want nothing to do with
to cop out
to back out after agreeing to take part in; or to take the easy way out. Also used as a noun
to argue the toss
to debate the finer details
to fartarse around
to fail to get on with the job in hand
hostile
angry
pissweak
term of derision for someone or something who is particularly lacking in admirable qualities
pline
"aeroplane" in Mediterstrinean

earyah
expression used when presenting someone with something
cop
(in this context) profit or share (Also known as a "sling".)
uppa shit crick
("up shit creek" in Mediterstrinean) in big trouble
turn it up
expression of derision
I dint come down inner larse share
another expression of derision, only longer
busted
arrested
like a bride's nightie
with all possible speed
D
a detective
cop shop
police station

Exercises

1. Name three instances where you could use the expression "earyah". Keep it clean.
2. Practise this sentence in Mediterstrinean: "The rine in Spine sties minely on the pline." Now get a job as a station announcer on the Eastern Suburbs train line in Sydney. Practise saying: "The trine on pletform ite and nine es come in sidewys."
3. What was in the bag? (a) Muesli (b) A vibrator (c) Marijuana (d) A jar of Vegemite.
4. If you answered (a) to question 3, put the book down, go into the lavatory and put your head down the bowl. Flush.

Expressing Preferences and Opinions

It is in expressing your preferences and opinions that you will best demonstrate your mastery of the Australian language. You will have absorbed quite a number of offensive descriptive terms from the preceding lessons, but here's a ready reference guide.

Just as there are many types of bastards, there are also many types of blokes and tarts. Blokes who are not all that bright are boofheads, drongos or mugs, and if you suspect their grip on reality is tenuous, they're not the full quid, they're a shingle short or they've got kangaroos in their top paddock.

If you also suspect that this condition is due to long periods of isolation or too much sun, you'll say they've "gone troppo".

A bloke who doesn't seem to know what he's about doesn't know if he's Arthur or Martha. Everything he does is all over the place like a mad woman's custard. This can be a temporary or a permanent condition. Such people often get things arse about face and anything they're involved with is very muddled and run on Rafferty's Rules.

If a person is lazy, they're a slackarse, and if they're a clown they're a bit of a dag. If clothes or decor are a bit tacky or poorly chosen, they're daggy.

A person who is extremely stupid is the biggest galah this side of the Black Stump (the Black Stump being a mythical post somewhere out in the bush that marks the last outpost of civilisation before the Great Culchral Desert — when you're this far away you're not within coo-ee).

If something is in poor taste it is a bit off, or a bit rough, and if it's very good it's magic, top stuff or mint, but often beaut or ripper. And if it's really special it's one out of the box.

Something that is not very good is not much chop, if it's worse it's not so hot, and if it's really bad it's up the shit or simply R.S. (ratshit). Or it can just be buggered or stuffed. If something is buggered or stuffed and it's your fault, you tubed it.

If you're tired you're rooted or buggered, and if you don't mind one way or the other you're easy. If you've got a lot of pluck you're as game as Ned Kelly and if you're audacious you've got a lot of front. Businessmen with a lot of front usually charge like wounded bulls.

If something is really getting you down it's a fair cow of a thing and if it's a piece of machinery it's a pig.

If someone tries to stop you having fun, they're a wowser (supposedly from the old credo: We Only Want Social Evils Remedied). If they're always borrowing cigarettes they smoke O.P.s (Other People's); if they're left-handed they're cack-handed; and if they're nosey they're a stickybeak.

If someone has the advantage they've got the wood on you, and if they've got a big advantage they have you by the short and curlies or the short hairs.

Well I hope that gave you the drum, but if you still don't know whether you're Arthur or Martha then I reckon you wouldn't get a kick in a stampede.

17

Starting a Business

Mr Foster is as happy as a pig in shit. He's just got a cheque for ten grand from Lotto. He's down the pub chewing the fat with Davo.

Instant Conversation

LES: You wooden read about it. I've ad all these angers-on brown-nosin up ter me all week. Summa the jokers I never seen before.

DAVO: Got some front some people, eh?

LES: Bloody oath. Jeez, it's beaut not avin ter worry about money for a bit. Your shout.

(Davo buys two more middies.)

DAVO: (mutters) Tight as a fish's arse.

LES: Eh?

DAVO: I said I like the barmaid's arse.

LES: Yeah, right.

DAVO: Les . . . wodya gunna do with alla that money?

LES: Ardunno. Why?

DAVO: I'm thinkina startin me own biz. Just short of a bita the necessary, that's all.

LES:	Jeez, another suckhole.
DAVO:	Eh, fair go. I'm yer mate, remember? Oo got ya the brickeyin job?
LES:	Come off the grass.
DAVO:	All I'm sayin is we could be partners. I jus need a few bob for a ute an a bita gear an we'd shit it in. Think of it — our own show. My brawn — your brains — we gotta be in front. Probly double the ten grand inner first three months!
LES:	(interested) Yer reckon?

Vocabulary

happy as a pig in shit
very happy. A more polite form of the expression is "happy
as Larry"
chewing the fat
having a long, leisurely chat
you wooden read about it
expression of disbelief and/or amázement
hangers-on
sycophants
brown-nosing
behaving in an ingratiating manner
bloody oath
that is absolutely correct
beaut
very common Australian expression for anything that is very
good
tight as a fish's arse
miserly. (Also "mean as cat's piss".) Such people are also said
to be "miserable bastards"
fair go
be reasonable. Said while going up and down through an
octave for the right musical effect. A more colourful form
is "fair suck of the sav", but this is no longer in common usage
come off the grass
an expression of derision

to shit it in
to do something very easily

Exercises

1. Will Davo and Les shit it in? Keep your answer brief (no more than two letters).
2. If you were Les what would you do with the money? (a) Piss it up the wall (b) Invest it in futures (c) Buy some marijuana plants and relocate to Griffith (d) Buy a week's non-stop sensual experience at the Pink Pussy Massage Parlour.
3. If you answered (b) write "I've just done my dough" a hundred times.

L'1 L'8

Announcing an Engagement

Darlene is having it off with a rich kid from the North Shore. His name is Marshall. His surname is also Marshall. Darlene and Marshall Marshall have decided to get hitched, and he's just broken the news to his oldies. They are not rapt.

Marshall's old man is top of the wozzer at some oil company. He's an elitist shit with a house in Mosman and more money than you could poke a stick at.

Instant Conversation

MRS MARSHALL: I'm awake up to the ungry little bitch. She's on the make, a course. She lives in some grotty little place in Darlingurst. Imagine. An she's gotta rug-rat as well.

MR MARSHALL: Well e's done is dash now. Iffy marries the slut e's not gettin another cent off me.

MRS MARSHALL: E's away with the pixies arf the time, that's is trouble.

MR MARSHALL: Suppose we get this tart to one side — tell er we think they're both too young, blah de blah . . . then see if we can buy er off?

MRS MARSHALL: Miteswell give it a burl, I spose.

MR MARSHALL:	Really put the acid on — see if she bites.
MRS MARSHALL:	An if she doesn't?
MR MARSHALL:	We'll just avter cop it sweet. (pause) I wonder what the rest of er family's like?

Vocabulary

having it off with
having an affair with
North Shore
the north shore of Sydney harbour. A prestige address
rapt
excited or pleased
top of the wozzer
number one man
elitist
Nouveau Oz for "snob"
more money than you could poke a stick at
a great deal of money
to be awake up to
to be fully aware of another's motivations and intentions
hungry
selfish, mean or grasping. Often used as an adjective to describe land developers and taxi drivers
on the make
looking for material profit or sexual conquest
rug-rat
a baby
to do one's dash
to go too far
away with the pixies
daydreaming. Describes someone who is not fully conversant with reality
blah de blah
etcetera, etcetera
to give it a burl
to give it a try (Also "have a lash".)
to put the acid on
to put to the test

to see if she bites
to discover if the victim will take the bait
to cop it sweet
to accept it manfully

Exercises

1. Should Darlene take the money or go on and try for the car?
2. Name five things you could poke a stick at.

$L'1 \; L'9$

Going to a Wedding

Marshall has his buck's night the night before the wedding. The dillbrains he is with get him on the slops and put him on a train. He's out to it and ends up somewhere at the back of Bourke. He only just makes it back in time.

At the wedding Mr Foster asks Marshall's father if he wants to kick in for a pressie, but Mr Marshall can't even crack it for a smile. Darlene is sweating on her old man behaving himself but Blind Freddie can see what's going to happen.

Mr Foster is already half-cut when he gets to the reception. He's very much on the outer and Marshall's oldies treat him with ignore. He hops into the booze and pretty soon he's nice and untidy. Meanwhile Mrs Marshall is earbashing one of the guests.

Instant Conversation

MRS MARSHALL: (to a guest) I dint mind im slummin it for a while. But I dint think e'd end up marryin the little tart.

(Les overhears this. It's like a red rag to a bull.)

LES: Doan rubbish my Darlene, y'old cow!

(Mrs Marshall screams. Mr Marshall comes over.)

MR MARSHALL: Wossgowinon?

MRS MARSHALL: E called me a cow!

LES:	Not worth a pincha goat shit, the lot a youse!
MR MARSHALL:	Mind yer language. There's ladies present.
LES:	(pretending to strain his eyes) Where?
SHANE:	Good value. Go for it, dad!

Mr Foster decides to mix it, and there is a shemozzle. He finally gets up on the bridal table, drops his daks, and chucks a browneye.

Vocabulary

buck's night
a stag party
dillbrains
idiots
on the slops
drinking alcohol with the intention of getting inebriated
out to it
unconscious, either through exhaustion or alcohol-induced stupor
back of Bourke
in the middle of nowhere. Bourke is a town in New South Wales standing right on the edge of the Culchral Desert, which is a barren waste extending from Bourke in the east, to Perth in the west
to kick in for a pressie
to contribute towards the purchase of a gift (Also known as "chipping in".)
can't crack it for a smile
is unable to see the humour in a situation
to sweat on
to be anxious about
Blind Freddie
fictitious character who is able to anticipate the obvious in advance of real people with 20/20 vision
half-cut
drunk

on the outer
persona non grata
to treat someone with ignore
to give someone the cold shoulder
to hop into the booze
to start drinking at a rapid rate
untidy
drunk, usually raucously
to earbash
to enjoin someone in conversation without allowing them
opportunity to participate also. A person who habitually
engages in earbashing is known as a "lug-punisher"
to slum it
to go out with someone who is one's physical or social inferior
little tart
a girl with loose morals. "Tart" is not a term of abuse; "little
tart" is another matter
a red rag to a bull
an incitement to violent behaviour
to rubbish
to insult, or put down
not worth a pinch of goat shit
worthless
good value
an expression of extreme approval
go for it
an expression of encouragement, usually uttered by someone
who intends to stand back and watch
to mix it
to fight
shemozzle
(peculiar Jewish entry into the language) a scuffle or a
commotion
daks
trousers
to chuck a browneye
to bend over and bare one's hinder parts, spreading the
glutimus maximus muscles simultaneously. This is usually
done to demonstrate to the onlookers that you have a low
opinion of them

Exercises

1. Go into the front yard and chuck a browneye. Write down your neighbours' reactions.
2. Do you think Les was justified in resorting to violence to protect Darlene's honour? (a) Yairs (b) Nar (c) Only if the other bloke was smaller than he was.

2

We Say Goodbye to the Family

The business has gone down the gurgler and Mr Foster has done his dough. He jumped in, boots an' all, and Davo racked off with the capital. Mr Foster is absolutely ropeable. He's been left with stuff all. He's decided to move to the Gong and work for his brother, stitching up wood ducks in a car yard.

Shane has really come a gutzer. Enzo and Aaron have skipped bail and left Shane to be the bunny. If the jury accepts the verbals he'll end up getting the rough end of the pineapple. He's thinking of spilling his guts and dobbing them both in.

Darlene reckons it's really stiff about Shane, but life must go on. She's really clucky, with another sprog on the way. Marshall and Darlene and baby Gayle have gone alternative and live in the bush growing veggies. Marshall is really down on his old man but is being very supportive of Darlene. They're really into personal growth and spend a lot of time having in-depth conversations with really meaningful dialogue. They are being really up front with each other.

Mrs Foster has had it with Mr Foster. He has really queered his pitch with her and the brickeying business was the killer. She's decided to wipe the lot of them and is planning to meet Davo at Surfer's. They plan to fly over to Freo and make a big quid selling T-shirts to the Yanks during the America's Cup.

We hope you have enjoyed meeting the Foster family. Perhaps we will meet them again sometime soon. Hoo-roo.

113

Vocabulary

to go down the gurgler
to fail dramatically
to do one's dough
to lose one's money
boots an' all
wholeheartedly
ropeable
extremely angry (Also "spitting chips".)
stuff all
nothing
the Gong
Wollongong. A town with little charm to recommend it, 80
km south of Sydney
to stitch up a wood duck
to dupe a gullible person
to come a gutzer
to be overtaken by disaster
bunny
fall guy
verbals
uncorroborated evidence submitted by the police
to get the rough end of the pineapple
to get a raw deal
to spill one's guts
to confess
to dob someone in
to give evidence that will incriminate that person
stiff
bad luck (Also "rugged".)
clucky
the state where one's mothering instinct is highly visible
sprog
(short for sproggett) offspring
alternative
adjective denoting those who have taken up an alternative
lifestyle to that offered in the city. Most become muesli
farmers in Nimbin
really down on
Nouveau Oz for "angry with"

supportive
Nouveau Oz for "nice to", often used in reference to men who are not shirking their responsibilities as fathers
personal growth
self indulgence
in-depth conversation
two people indulging themselves
dialogue
Nouveau Oz for "conversation"
up front
(Nouveau Oz) honest to the point of rudeness
to have had it with
to be fed up with
to queer one's pitch
to perform acts that lessen one's personal standing in the eyes of another person
killer
the straw that broke the camel's back
wipe
exorcise from the mind
Surfer's
Surfers Paradise. Popular Queensland summer resort consisting of hotels and a beach
Freo
Fremantle. A port in Western Australia
big quid
a lot of money
hoo-roo
goodbye

Exercises

1. Did you know right from the start that Shane would come a gutzer? You smug bastard.
2. What do you think of Davo's form? Be moralistic.
3. If you still haven't got a feel for the language, buy a pineapple, find the rough end and insert it rectally. You have just got the rough end of the pineapple.
4. Locate your wife and children. Ring them up if you have to. Be supportive for five minutes.

Graduation

1. Understanding the Australian Joke

There was me and Gazza, doin nashos down at Puckapunyal,
dint see a tart for two months, all the blokes were angin out
for a root. So finely wunna the officers comes in an says:
"Okay youse blokes, we're gunna do the right thing, we've
lined up some talent."

Everyone says: "Oh, you little ripper! Makes a change from
pullin the pud." Next day we all choof off inner truck, right
out inter the scrub, backa Bourke somewhere.

Finely we bundle out an the officer points to an erda camels
an says: "Orright fellas — go for it," an everyone starts leggin
it after these camels.

I says to Gazza: "Wait on, stuffin camels! What are we
all runnin for?"

E says: "Well — yer doan wanna get an *ugly* one, do ya?"

---

*If your response to this instruction was to say "Officious bastard"
or "Come off the grass", you have begun to think like an Australian
and may collect your diploma now.

Questions
1. What is the point of the joke?
2. Describe an ugly camel.
3. What is Puckapunyal? (a) A place in Victoria (b) A sort of vegetable (c) A sort of camel.

2. Understanding the Pommy Joke

Q: What's the difference between a pongo and a computer?
A: You have to punch information into both of them, but with a computer you only have to do it once.

Questions:
1. What is a pongo?
2. What is a computer?

3. Understanding the Stupid Australian Joke

Bloke goes to this station, an in wunna the paddocks there's this pig, see, an it's only got three legs. E says: "Wossa matter with that pig?" And the cockie says: "Doan rubbish that pig. That pig's a gun—it can shear 200 sheep in a day."

The bloke says: "Yeah, it's only got three legs but." An the cockie says: "Look, that pig's a little ripper. It can muster cattle better than a kelpie."

The bloke says: "Yeah, but why's it only got three legs?" The cockie says: "That pig's nobody's bunny, I'll give ya the drum. It can crutch 50 lambs, get a feeda yabbies from the dam and cook up a damper for tea, all in an arvo."

The bloke says: "Yeah, but wait on, why's it only got three legs?" An the cockie says: "Well—when a pig's that shit-hot, yer doan eatim all at once."

Questions:
1. Did you understand this joke? (a) Yairs (b) Nar.
2. If you answered (a), go back to the beginning and start again.
3. If (b) you graduate with honours. Congratulations.